W9-CSE-356

HOW TO
OUTSMART
YOUR BRAIN

Using Your Emotions to Make the
Best Decisions...*At Work*

MARCIA REYNOLDS

Published by: Covisioning
www.covisioning.com

Copyright © 2002 by Marcia Reynolds

All rights reserved. No part of this book may be reproduced or transmitted in any form whatsoever, electronic or mechanical, without written permission from Covisioning, except for brief quotations attributed to Marcia Reynolds embodied in articles or reviews.

Published by:
Covisioning
4301 N. 21st St. #56
Phoenix, AZ 85016
602-954-9030
Fax: 602-553-3791
marcia@covisioning.com

First edition
ISBN: 0-9655250-4-X

Editor: Kate von Seeburg

Book cover, interior design and production: Michele O'Hagan, Masterpiece Publishing, LLC, Phoenix, Arizona

Back cover photo: John Hall

Printed in the United States of America

How to order:
Copies may be ordered from Covisioning.
Quantity discount available by calling 602-954-9030.
Visit us online at *www.covisioning.com* for updates and articles.

CONTENTS

PREFACE

A NEW PARADIGM
FOR CHANGE

I watched a world-renowned expert on relationships answer questions from a talk show audience. A woman volunteered to be coached on her problem. She admitted taunting her husband during fights, picking at him where he was most vulnerable. She knew this wasn't fighting fairly, but she couldn't stop. The expert said, "Yes you can. Just stop." The woman sat down a bit bewildered and totally embarrassed. I knew her problem would persist.

We have been hearing for years, "Change your thoughts, you change your behavior." Yet affirmations rarely change our habits, especially when our buttons get pushed into anger and our minds are flooded with fear. In the end, the mantra "Just do it" has created more guilt than success. People wonder why they are so weak that they just can't do it — change their diet, speak up to their boss, ask their spouse for what they really need — and either live in self-loathing or resign themselves to living less than their potential. Even those who idolize the motivation masters find themselves having to play the Tony Robbins tape daily or quote Dr. Phil to their friends to force themselves to stay on track.

What's missing? I taught these same techniques for years, then often called myself a fraud for not practicing what I preached in the heat of the moment. When my emotions took over, my logic disappeared. Even when I tried the latest techniques in meditating, simplifying my life and visualizing white lights around my nemesis, I still had a breaking point beyond which there was no return.

Then I discovered the concept of emotional intelligence when I read Daniel Goleman's book, *Emotional Intelligence.* As I delved into the research, I discovered that there was a Wizard of Oz controlling my mind behind the curtains. To my relief, I found I could pull back those curtains and take control of my reactions. The emotions didn't go away. I just learned ways in which to recognize when they appeared and shift them before they flooded my consciousness. Then I could practice my self-talk regimen.

I now teach my workshop Accessing Emotional Intelligence^SM to people of various backgrounds and cultures. Those who are most resistant — who shudder at the thought of discussing feelings — generally become my greatest champions by the end of the class. The reason? They finally experience what it feels like to be free. If we don't deal with our emotions, they hold us in contempt, sabotaging our perspective, our decision-making, our relationships, and our happiness. If we learn how to acknowledge them when they appear, we are better able to connect with others, and feel more peacefulness and joy in our lives.

This short book will introduce you to the path. As you practice the techniques, you will gain an incredible wealth of knowledge about yourself. Although the context is how to use emotional intelligence at work, the new mental habits you create will help improve the quality of your personal life as well. My greatest reward is the e-mail and cards I get from those I teach. They share with me what they learned at home as well as on the job after they leave my classroom. In turn, I learn more. I'm honored to share with you some of the wisdom they have helped me to uncover.

CHAPTER 1

■

TO FEEL OR
NOT TO FEEL

In my last corporate position, I was hired as the organizational training manager for a semiconductor corporation, responsible for creating programs in leadership development, personal effectiveness and
team success. After six months, my boss told me the company had
decided that I should also manage all aspects of factory training.

I balked.

I had no clue about what went on in the factory. I had no previous
experience in this industry and I had successfully evaded anything in
my education that could be termed technical. I also knew that the
department had been bumped from being managed by manufacturing, then from process engineering, and finally from human resources
before it ended up in my lap. This had to be a drain on the morale of
the trainers. My boss answered my concerns by saying, "Don't worry.
It's a no-brainer. It's just three women who come to work, do their
jobs, then go home."

The hair on my back bristled. When was managing anyone a "no-
brainer?" I reluctantly accepted the responsibility, hoping to provide
the three trainers with a more permanent home.

Planning to employ the techniques I taught in my management
classes, I scheduled an appointment with each of the trainers. The first
trainer, Cathy, came into my office. As she sat, I asked, "So tell me,
what is your vision?"

She looked confused.

I explained, "You know, what do you want for yourself in your
job? Is there anything you'd like to learn? How would you like to
develop yourself? Is there something you'd like to do more of or less
of on the job?"

She thought about my questions, then said, "There's a new computer system on the floor. I'd love to create some new reporting forms. What we have is so outdated. It would help us a lot if we had a better way to track people and what they're doing."

"Great," I said. "What's it going to take? How can I help?"

"There's a class I can take. I can sign up if you approve the overtime." We worked out the schedule.

Dina, the second trainer came into my office. Again I asked, "So tell me, what is your vision?"

She looked confused.

I explained, "What do you want for yourself? How would you like to develop and grow? Is there something you'd like to do more of or less of on the job?"

She thought about the question, shifted her body a few times, then sheepishly said, "I'd like to be a supervisor."

"Great," I said. "What's it going to take? How can I help?"

"I'm not sure."

"Can you ask some of your supervisors on the floor what they think?"

"Sure."

"Good. Find out, then we can work out a plan together." She came back a week later with a detailed plan of training and a commitment by one of the factory supervisors to mentor her development.

The third trainer, Sandy, came into my office. I skipped the vision question. "How would you like to develop yourself? Is there something you'd like to do more or less of on the job?"

She thought about the question, then shut her eyes. Tears began to roll down her cheeks. Finally, she said, "I've worked here 16 years. That's the first time anyone asked me that."

Do you think these trainers acted as my boss had described them, as people who came to work, did their job, then left?

Hardly. My greatest problem was managing their overtime. Cathy was rewarded for her new reporting system, Dina became the company's first factory training supervisor, and Sandy committed herself to a personal development program that she claimed brought her back from the "living dead." The high evaluations they received from those they trained reflected their renewed motivation to work.

The point of the story is not to tout my success. Success should be given to the management programs I had been teaching over the years; I was just practicing what I taught. The point is that the difference in these employees' productivity had nothing to do with their knowledge and skills. The bottom line was impacted by their emotional commitment. Their performance was based on how they felt while doing the job, not on how well they knew how to do it.

It's a simple formula. I WANT TO do a good job, so I do. I DON'T FEEL LIKE doing a good job, so I don't, at least not to my maximum potential.

No matter how strong my work ethic is, when factors in my environment detract from *how good I feel* when I'm working, the result is a decrease in the energy available to perform. Other factors, such as *anger, anxiety* or *determination* may motivate me for a while, but sooner or later I will have to feel *pride* in my work, *valued* by my supervisors and *acknowledged* by my peers in order to maintain my motivation to work at my peak.

Notice that every italicized word in the above paragraph indicates an emotion. This concept suggests that the success of a company rests on the emotions felt by the employees.

■ THE SEEDS OF DISCONTENT

The power of I WANT TO in the workforce overrides great marketing plans and brilliant innovations. This isn't news. We've known for years that motivation is critical to productivity. Then why don't we have a better handle on managing emotions in the workplace?

In my 20 years of experience working with corporations, government agencies, and not-for-profit associations, I have found across the board two reasons that managers fail in their ability to touch their employees at an emotional level:

1. They don't know how.
2. They don't have the desire to learn how.

The result: One study found 27% of employees are so unhappy they sabotage tasks and steal from their employers while 60% come to work just to get a paycheck. Only 13% are happily committed to doing an excellent job.

Have we always experienced this state of unrest?

Many long-term managers tell me, "No, people once were happy to have a paycheck and worked hard out of personal pride." This may or may not be true but I do know that a significant shift is underway in the business environment: Workers no longer want to be managed.

Where once fear may have been a motivator to work hard, it now deflates morale, causes either increased turnover or decreased productivity, and in the end, can destroy an organization.

Why has the change in focus occurred? A number of reasons play into the situation, including a decrease in the skilled labor market, economic uncertainty, a generation that watched their parents' growing displeasure and trust in the companies they worked for, a workforce that is cognizant of the words "respect" and "self-care," and the shift from an industrial to informational, people-centered workplace.

Let's look at a few of these factors.

Considering the labor market, in 1975 we had the fewest number of babies born per 1000 than in all recorded history. In a growing economy, this decreases the number of qualified workers. In times of economic downturn, a shrinking labor market forces more competition for star performers. To make matters worse, thousands of people over 45, with 20 percent of them senior managers and executives, are leaving to start their own businesses. Even in the midst of the heavy layoffs in 2001, retention of skilled employees continued to be a major problem for employers. According to a survey by Manchester, Inc. and Accounting Principles, nearly 100 firms said their monetary-related retention methods were failing.

Therefore, the opportunity to grow an organization is limited by the ability to recruit and retain talent. Money may attract, but can't keep employees who can earn the same pay down the street. Since the 1960s, studies have shown that career development, positive work challenges, and feelings of personal contribution and achievement outweigh compensation as the top factors considered when the average knowledge worker chooses an employer.

In 1994, Walker Research in Indianapolis found that "employee treatment" was by far the most important consideration by individuals choosing a place to work and those deciding whether or not to stay on the job. In fact, the Gallup Organization found that immediate supervisors had the largest influence on an employee's decision to quit. Employees left a company because of how they felt about their managers, not due to the nature of their jobs or the state of the company.

One woman claimed she left her dream job in the film industry because she didn't feel appreciated. She said she might have stayed if the boss bought dinner once in a while when the team had to work late. "I left for want of a thank you and a hamburger," she said.

This translates to the fact that employees stay because their managers create a place they "like," largely an emotional decision. This may also mean that whereas employees may not have loyalty to a company, they may feel loyalty to a manager.

At the executive level, McKinsey & Company found that 58 percent of senior managers join and stay with a company because they feel their values are in alignment with those of the company's culture. Factors also rated high include freedom and autonomy, exciting job challenges, and public acknowledgment of management success. Lowest on the list were compensation and geographic location.

In short, people decide to stay or leave based on emotional issues. Even if they stay, the amount of energy employees put into the job is based more on how they feel than what they are paid.

You may be shaking your head at this moment saying, "So what's new? I know this already." Yet even in companies that acknowledge that employees must be treated differently than in the past, few changes have had a permanent effect in the way people are managed. Employees have heard talk, but have not seen action. They are looking for changes in the behavior of their supervisors, for their managers to "walk their talk." They are justly dissatisfied with the progress.

What do employees want?

Simply, they want what they have been promised — more responsibility, more freedom, more power, and more accountability.

What they are getting instead is direction, coordination, explanations on occasion, more work dumped on them when they perform, evaluation with little reward, and discipline.

Although we know these practices impede growth especially when organizations are crying for more creativity, innovation, and risk-taking, no time is given to effect the necessary changes. Everyone is overwhelmed with the demands of work. Who has time for training and trying on behaviors that could fail? Yet the change is essential in today's competitive, fast-moving world.

According to an article in the *Wall Street Journal*, May 2001, the growth of the role of technology in our economy has intensified the problem. The lack of people skills and business sense in technical wizards has created "nerd bosses from hell." Their arrogance and impatience drive top performers out the door and breed resentment and insecurity in employees who stay.

The problem isn't confined to the technological sectors. Sales teams, support staff and front line operations in most companies act more like dysfunctional families than work units. The companies that continue to give top priority to financial performance will have the most difficult time staying alive.

Fortunately for our economy, a growing number of organizations are now convinced that people's ability to understand and to manage their emotions improves their performance, their collaboration with colleagues and their interaction with customers. The leaders of these organizations know that whether we are talking about a tight labor market, an economic downturn or the problem of lackluster perform-ance in lame-duck employees near retirement, managers can no longer ask, "What do I want them to do?" Now they MUST ask, "How do I want them to feel?"

■ Emotions and the Bottom Line

I've been teaching employee training programs for 20 years, all focused on showing respect in our communications and providing a sense of significance to those we work with. If we have been teaching the correct skills for years, why haven't they taken hold?

In my experience, the programs teach concepts at an intellectual level. We've been asking people to change their behavior by showing them what to do and asking them to be disciplined with their practice.

This works for a day or two after they attend a class but as soon as they are up against the wall with outrageous deadlines, angry cus-tomers and stupid colleagues, they forget what they learned. They revert to their old behavior. The investment in training is lost.

Studies prove that within a week after attending a class teaching behavioral skills, only 10% of information is retained. Is this statistic static, due to the workings of the human brain? Or can we increase retention and the possibilities of lasting behavioral change?

One factor in retention is that back on the job where the changes need to take place, we are dealing with emotions at two levels: the emotions of employees and the emotions of the managers trying to effect the emotions of employees.

If change must take place at an emotional level, then we have to in-clude the emotional elements of behavioral change in our training as well.

However, when it comes to dealing with emotions, most people don't know where or how to begin. We grow up in cultures that dis-miss the need to understand emotions; individual technical achievement is emphasized in schools and is used as the basis for promotions at work. Emotions do not show up in the language of report cards, performance reviews, and action plans except for those veiled as a "poor attitude" and "low morale."

As a result, employees and managers are not only poorly trained in getting along others, but their focus on the technical and intellectual factors of work may actually hinder success by limiting possibilities.

Yet the solution goes much further than training people in the foreign language of emotions. The totality of the individual, feelings and all, must be taken into consideration at all levels of corporate decision-making in order to embed the importance in the corporate culture. Every employee, from the bottom to the top, needs to learn how to speak, write, listen and interact with emotional intelligence.

■ A Cultural Concern

Count how many times a day you talk to others at work, or depend on the outcomes of others to get your work done. Multiply this number by 200 for every year you are in business. You'll see that you have thousands of interactions, many of them taxing your interpersonal skills. Your success on the job is dependent on your ability to work with and through others.

Add your increasing responsibilities to the equation. You have been asked to do twice the work to produce three times the results. This equates to at least four times the problems with interpersonal relationships and stress.

Working an average of 67 hours a week, we barely have time to think about our relationships, with little energy to work on improving them. It's no wonder the numbers of people depressed and angry on the job are growing.

Business as usual won't do. To stay alive, organizations need to include building relationships and emotional inspiration in their strategic plans. Conversations that reveal values and needs must be infused in our hiring and promoting procedures. Cultures must shift to honor discussions that include emotional factors.

When emotional intelligence was taught to a group of sales agents at the Minneapolis-based American Express insurance division, (specifically, they were taught to be more aware of their emotions, were given tools to change negative emotions into positive ones, and were provided methods to identify and design their work to align with the specific personal values that motivated them at work), nearly 90 percent reported significant improvements in their sales performance, adding tens of millions of dollars in revenue. One participant described the process as "giving people the permission, language, and structure for bringing their entire self to work."

Studies like this are confirming the importance of being present to the moment — to oneself and to others — to find ways to make work more challenging, interesting, and fun in a safe and supportive environment. Soft skills, once defined as employee perks in times of growth, are now essential building blocks for long-term success. No longer can people be treated like hired hands. The evidence confirms that people should be allowed to bring their hearts with them to work as well.

CHAPTER 2

■

CLUELESS IN
THE WORKPLACE

I start my class Accessing Emotional Intelligence℠ by asking participants to name an animal they identify with and why. If they can't
identify an animal (some have difficulty with this exercise), then I ask
them to describe themselves as a weather pattern. The key to this exercise is the depth they go into when describing the animal or the
weather in terms of their own behavior. I may have to goad the first few
participants to explain how the metaphor fits their personality. After
that, most people jump into the exercise, easily describing how they are
as moody as a Siamese cat or as volatile as a summer thunderstorm.

Following the exercise, I ask the class how many participants
would have described themselves as moody or volatile had I asked
them to simply describe their behavior at work. All agree that they
would have stuck to words such as "friendly," or "focused," picking
only socially-acceptable terms without going into depth, details or
even the truth.

I had to create a vehicle for them to reveal aspects about themselves. It's difficult to get people to speak about "who" they are at
work, even in a class entitled, "Accessing Emotional Intelligence.℠"
Yet given an impersonal platform, it appears that people do like to talk
about themselves and will allow themselves to be vulnerable, admit-
ting to traits that aren't necessarily positive, even in a room full of
strangers.

What animal or weather pattern describes you at work? Write
your answer down, giving details of your behavior. This is your first
step to self-awareness.

The reason my course starts with the word "accessing" is because
as a by-product of living with others as we grow and mature, we all

develop an intelligence about how our feelings affect our decisions and actions. In fact, children seem to have a great curiosity around learning what makes them happy and sad. Toddlers are particularly sensitive to the feelings of others before they learn how to speak. Yet, as we become more socially aware, we depend less on our emotional intelligence and more on the societal rules we are taught by our parents, teachers and peers. We even distrust and ignore the messages we get from the emotional centers of our brain. Specifically in the workplace:

1. We don't heed what our "gut" tells us to do.
2. We're cautioned not to "let your heart rule your mind."
3. We've been taught to have a "stiff upper lip" and not to reveal our emotions because they make us look weak.

The result is that we create habits that block our ability to use emotional information when we make decisions and communicate with others. Ask most people how they feel and they say, "Fine." Some say it with no emotion. Others reveal their true state in the inflection and volume of their voice. Yet few people actually stop to assess their condition. Of those who would, most would think twice before telling the truth unless they were feeling absolutely marvelous. Even the ones who would love to express how upset they are in the moment, choose to remain tight-lipped, secretly hoping the asker will sense the pain and show remorse.

At work, courses in interpersonal competence focus on developing skills in problem solving, such as conflict resolution, change management and team building. They are generally limited to one-day "fix-it" programs. Managers rarely show up. The participants who do attend are taught communication skills at an intellectual level, with the advice to set their emotions aside. When they return to the job, they might try out a skill or two. Then, when under pressure, they return to their former habits.

The fault is placed on the trainer or program. Some courses may be offered in stress management and self-esteem to help cope with the pressures, but they are generally considered "fluff" to demonstrate that the company cares about their well being.

I rarely find a company interested in the investment needed to train and coach their employees to recognize their emotions on the job. Even fewer are companies concerned about increasing happiness.

Most people don't even have the literacy to define how they feel if they were asked. We understand the meaning of the words academically, but have difficulty defining what we are experiencing in ourselves at any given moment. Prior to attending my class, I have the participants fill out the survey that is included in Appendix A, "Taking Stock of Your Emotions." At four intervals throughout the day, they are told to stop and write 1) what they are doing and 2) how they are feeling, choosing from the list of 80 possible emotions. Most say that they struggle with selecting the words. They dislike the number of choices and can't differentiate one type of happiness, fear or anger from another.

The good news is that after only a few days, the exercise is easier. They begin to identify subtle distinctions in their reactions. Patterns emerge. They can say, "I feel confused, delighted, frustrated, embarrassed or exhausted" without looking at the list. They feel more in control simply by taking the time to check in with themselves. And this awareness is only the first step. Once they become fluent at identifying their emotions, they can apply a number of different techniques to shift negative emotions to more positive ones if they choose to. A few of these techniques are identified later in this book.

■ EMOTIONAL INTELLIGENCE AND CHOICE

Although researchers have actually identified about a dozen intelligences, Daniel Goleman, author of *Emotional Intelligence,* claims emotional intelligence to be the greatest predictor of social satisfaction and success in life.

In business, a manager's success depends on first understanding what is at the source of his or her own behavior and mental reactions before they can clearly interpret those of someone else. And even when you master awareness, knowing how to manage your reactions to your emotions once you are aware of their presence takes dedicated practice and persistence to overcome a lifetime of the habit of letting your brain run in cruise control.

So once a person is "alert" to his or her emotional reactions, the second competency defined as "emotional intelligence" is self-management. One of the problems we face in the workplace is the definition given to the word "management."

In the past, self-management was synonymous with self-control and the suppression of emotions, yet when speaking of being emotionally intelligent, self-management actually means demonstrating "choice." In fact, the root of the word "intelligent" is *legere* which means "choosing" and *inter* meaning "between." When emotionally intelligent, a person evaluates a situation in such a way that he or she sees there are options in how a situation can be viewed, and thus options in the possible reactions.

Self-management is then defined as the choice a person makes between options on how to feel at any particular moment, with one choice hopefully to react to the situation in such a way that enhances performance and interactions. The choice that most relates to creativity and peak performance is *to feel good*. However, in my experience, suggesting a corporate goal of having everyone *feel good* would generate a loud "humbug."

When I wrote my book, *Capture the Rapture,* a book about choosing joy, I was aware that it would not appeal to the corporate mindset. I've been accused of being touchy-feely enough in my career to know that topics that don't promise success, win-win outcomes, or highly effective strategies are suspect.

Yet according to Goleman's findings on the neurophysiology of the brain, the utmost goal we should strive to achieve is happiness. When the body experiences pleasure, the blood freely circulates through the brain feeding creativity and clearing the way to focus on the task at hand. The serotonin released with joy activates the greatest level of mental activity. We learn best when we are having fun. We are most alive when we are happy. We seek to do our best, and strive to repeat the circumstances that created the happiness over and over in our lives.

All other emotions — fear, anger, frustration, stress, disappointment, resentment, even contentment — constrict or slow circulation, either diverting blood to the large muscle groups or slowing the metabolism, shrinking the capacity to think. We see fewer options, if any at all. We can only focus on one thing at a time. It is rare when a person can engage the power of happiness under adverse conditions. For those who react with negative stress, the adversity paralyzes their brains, with fear flooding the creative center. We may produce when we are afraid or angry but our brain tends to narrow-in instead of expanding.

The brain can only maintain intensity fed by adrenalin for short periods of time unless helped by chemicals such as caffeine. Eventually, the body needs a rest. It will force the recess through illness if the person doesn't choose to take time out on his or her own.

The irony is that in the attempt to deny emotions, we only impede the positive emotions, including happiness and passion, which further perpetuates emotions of fear, disappointment and anger that clog creativity and restrict productivity.

So why isn't happiness ever a factor in strategic plans?

Most often, leaders declare that work is not a place for having fun. They falsely believe that there is a state of "no emotion" and they don't understand that suppressing or rationalizing emotions is not the same as having no emotions. It only means that the person uses their brain to stop feeling the emotion that is present, *for now.*

As humans, we are always in a state of emotion. If we deny the existence, we lose access to the information conveyed by the energy of the emotion. This information is rarely understood out of context. If you can be present to an emotion in the moment, you may be able to determine the source and choose your reaction. If the moment passes, the data about the emotion gets lost behind other information vying for our attention. Sooner or later, suppressed negative emotions seek to be released. When negative emotions find their way out, the information it could have provided gets confused with the prevailing situation. Angry emotions get misplaced, focused on blaming other people or situations, or in self-denigration which poisons our health.

Wouldn't you rather have the option of releasing your emotions than to stuff them, leaving it to chance how they affect you?

Being present to the information conveyed by our emotions affects performance levels, relationships, health, satisfaction with our work, and ultimately, our satisfaction with life.

This doesn't mean you have to express your emotions at work. It only means that you allow the possibility that they exist. In so doing, you can learn to identify when emotions show up, then make a conscious choice about how you want to react.

■ THE ART OF SUPPRESSION

A team leader in my class told me he was afraid of turning his meetings into sensitivity groups. I told him that the point is not to share emotions for the sake of expression, but to better problem-solve and create.

The skill then is not how to manage the emotion, but rather how to manage the reaction to the emotions that naturally exist. The discussion may be uncomfortable, but may lead to greater results. For example, people find that they don't need to argue points endlessly and instead, choose to talk about why they are struggling to accept new ideas. Power struggles decrease. Meetings make more sense. More and lasting solutions emerge.

Another problem with suppression is that the brain does a poor job of sorting emotions. You can't learn how to suppress anger or fear without decreasing your ability to experience joy. Suppress one, you suppress them all. Life loses its color. Golda Meir said, "Those who don't know how to weep with their whole heart don't know how to laugh either."

One of the exercises I do in my Accessing Emotional Intelligence[SM] class is to have participants recount the events of the morning or previous weekend. Every ten seconds, they are given a different emotion to express as they tell the story, even if the words don't fit the emotion.

The trick is to be able to access their feelings without thinking about them, and act them out, actually release them, without worrying about what these feelings look like. If people pause to think, I ask them to speed up so they don't have time to think. With a little warming up, they actually experience a flood of emotion.

The point of the exercise is to begin to clear the channel to feeling while bypassing the censoring brain. With repeated practice, we become more aware of feelings as they occur, giving us a chance to explore why they occurred and what we need to ask for in order to release any negative hold they have on our perceptions.

During a class, one manager, Allen, spoke in a monotone. No matter how much I coaxed him, he refused to alter his expression. When he finished, he told me that he had learned to how to stay calm in all situations with no particular training. He did not seek training for himself, but to find a few ways to help those who worked for him to better deal with their emotions.

I commended him for his mastery, but asked if there was at least one person or situation that pushed his buttons. He said that nothing, not even an irate employee, bothered him. "I just handle it," he said. He explained that getting upset wasn't worth his time. He could better solve problems when he stayed neutral.

Again I commended him and agreed that a neutral tone improved conflict resolution. I asked him if he at least had a mentor or a good book that acted as his guide. I had never met anyone who had truly reached this level of consciousness without years of guidance and practice. I had to believe that although he probably let a lot of remarks roll of his back, some events and words had to hit him between the eyes.

He shook his head in denial.

"Let me ask you two more questions," I said. "If you still feel the same way about your temperament, then I'll admit to being wrong."

Allen agreed.

"You told us about taking your son to a soccer game. I gathered that he is a decent player. Can you tell me the last time that when he played so well that you burst out screaming and clapping for him?"

Allen sat quietly for a moment before he said, "It's been a few years."

"And when was the last time you rolled around on the floor with him, laughing so hard it hurt?" I asked.

This time his silence seemed like it went on forever. I resisted the urge to fill in the gap.

Finally, he said, "Okay, I got it."

Allen agreed to let me coach him privately after the class. We repeated the exercise many times over the next few weeks. Between sessions, he kept a log of experiences and a journal that helped him uncover how he felt about situations.

By the end of the month, Allen could tell his soccer story as if he were a Shakespearean actor.

He reported not only a richness returning to his home life, but a depth of new possibilities in both his work assignments and relationships.

Suppress one emotion, you hinder the ability to feel altogether. Whether the goal is to be a better manager, to be a better parent or to be a happier human, you must be present to what your heart is saying as well as your head. How many times do you smile during the day? Count them. You may be surprised by the result.

Success and happiness requires you be fully alive and present, aware of your emotions, their source, and their significance. Then you can choose the best course of action in the moment, to make a direct request or find a way to release the feelings and go on.

Becoming intimate with your emotions is the first step to feeling the freedom of choice in your life.

CHAPTER 3

■

WHAT IT TAKES TO BE
EMOTIONALLY INTELLIGENT

To become emotionally intelligent, you must 1) practice techniques that bring you into the present moment, then 2) identify your emotions, 3) determine the source of the emotion, and 4) choose how you want to react.

Your level of confidence and your level of energy in any given moment affect your ability to do the work; therefore, what you do to enhance your personal growth and decrease your stress will increase your ability to act with emotional intelligence.

With this in mind, there are four competencies:

1. Personal Foundation: Confidence and Capacity
2. Attention
3. Emotional Identification
4. Choice

1. PERSONAL FOUNDATION: CONFIDENCE AND CAPACITY

Many books and seminars are available to help you build your personal power and decrease stress levels. The first two chapters of my book, *Capture of the Rapture: How to Step Out of Your Head and Leap Into Life,* are devoted to helping the reader fill in the cracks of their foundations.

If you feel stressed, physically or mentally, it is difficult to be present, limiting your ability to act with intelligence. In contrast, the less stressed you are, the more you are able to intelligently analyze your emotions and your choices to react. A Self-Care Checklist is included in Appendix B at the end of this book. Raise your score and you raise your capacity for accessing emotional intelligence on a daily basis.

Skills development also includes:

— fostering a strong sense of purpose,
— creating a vision,
— reaching goals while managing priorities and time, and
— summoning the courage to question your assumptions and behavioral patterns.

A commitment to personal development goes a long way in creating the conditions that support your ability to analyze your emotional triggers and make good choices in response.

If you don't make this commitment, your progress will be excruciatingly slow. It's difficult enough staying present to the moment with all the external noises and demands on your time. Then you have a chatty brain well-trained to deceive you. As you will learn later in this chapter, the brain's primary function is to protect. It is always on the lookout for attackers. Therefore, the brain tends to see the world in a negative frame of reference. It's difficult to stay optimistic and positive with a brain that is biologically trained to be defensive.

It takes disciplined practice to outsmart your brain. You are changing long-term and ingrained thinking patterns, habits that are difficult to break. You must take care of yourself so that you can stay alert to your thinking and continually question whether your beliefs are useful and truthful. Only then can you get to the core of what is truly going on with your emotions to resolve problems and discover more meaningful solutions.

If you run your own organization or team, you might consider how strong is a person's foundation as a hiring/selection requirement. If you are working to increase your ability to access emotional intelligence, surrounding yourself with others who are also committed to raising theirs will support your efforts.

If you work with people who consider self-care as vital, who have a strong personal vision they are passionate about, who keep stress at a minimum, who know and honor their priorities in work and life, who are confident enough to ask for what they need appropriately and who have the courage to speak their minds as well as offer to help solve identified problems, then you'll find it easier to stay on a developmental path yourself.

If we honor and teach these competencies, we may be able to build emotionally intelligent cultures and communities.

2. ATTENTION

We humans are masters at zoning out. When someone is speaking to us, we smile, nod, say "uh-huh" and "hmm," while wondering if the front door is locked, planning dinner, and rehearsing our reply for when the person finally takes a breath. When on the phone, we are inspecting the lock on the door, inventorying the food available for dinner, and clearing out our e-mail message box. Amidst it all, one or two of the speaker's words may land in our consciousness, enabling us to dart into the present moment just long enough to keep the conversation going.

We can zone out practically anywhere and still survive. We become incognizant of our surroundings when working on repetitive tasks. How many drivers do you share the road with who are operating on automatic pilot? Think about this question the next time you opt not to fasten your seat belt.

The Internet operates in reverse. While logging on, we zone into cyberspace, lost to the world around us. Although surfing the Net may appear synonymous with being in the zone, it is not. When we hyper-focus, whether working, watching TV, or responding to a crisis, we tend to numb our emotions instead of sparking them.

What does it mean to "pay attention?"

It takes focusing ALL our senses in the present moment, something we are don't do well. We have to overcome decades of mental conditioning, yet the return on this investment is huge.

I found an enormous amount of research in the area of sports psychology on how to master this technique. In order for an athlete to be a champion, he or she must know how to "step into the zone" of the present. The best competitors do not think about anything, not even winning, that forces the possibility of losing. Instead, they allow their bodies to express how good it feels to be doing what they love.

The warm-up practices performed by professional athletes are intended to center their minds as well as their bodies. One golf pro told me that she used her "pre-shot routine" to feel in harmony with the present moment.

The techniques used by athletes can help you remain present to your life. Any time you catch yourself contemplating the past, fearing the future, or worrying about how others will judge you, you can deliberately alter your state of mind by practicing the following four steps:

a. Relax
b. Detach
c. Center
d. Focus

A. *RELAX*

Begin by relaxing your body. Tight muscles restrict blood flow to the brain. When blood flow is decreased, powerful emotions overrule logical thoughts, subjecting human behavior to a series of physiological responses. Daniel Goleman cites several physical responses to emotional states in *Emotional Intelligence*. Here are some of them:

— Anger directs blood to the hands, preparing the person to strike.
— Fear directs blood to the large muscles, mostly in the legs, preparing the person to flee.
— Sadness and disappointment decrease the metabolic rate, giving the person time to adjust to loss.
— Happiness directs blood to the brain, quieting worrisome thoughts, freeing up energy, and releasing overall good feelings.

Of these emotions, only happiness maximizes inactivity. If you are feeling anything other than happiness, you'll want to release the tension in your neck, back, arms and legs and stretch your muscles to stimulate the blood flow. You may chose to stay angry — anger can be a motivator to take risks and change — or even to grieve so you can move on. In order to make these choices rationally, you first need to relax your body.

There are many ways to relax. Try taking three long slow breaths, counting backward from 100 to 1 or stretching your tense muscles. For ongoing effects, deliberately slow down your life. Eat slowly, drive leisurely and walk at a gentle pace.

When pressures mount and you feel the adrenaline coursing through your veins, say, "STOP" and change your activity. Take a walk, read an article, send a note to a friend, or simply close your eyes and give thanks for being alive. If you're in the midst of a conversation or a meeting, STOP, breathe deeply and send your mind on a brief vacation. I imagine basking in a mountain pool looking up at the blue Arizona sky. No matter where I am, I can close my eyes and "go blue."

There are other techniques to shift your energy to release tension, such as doing anything to move your body, seeking out something that evokes your gratitude or love, and my favorite, finding something to laugh about.

If we are at our best mentally when we are happy, then how can we shift from frustration to fun? As they say, practice "looking at the bright side." If you make finding the lighter side of life a daily discipline, you may train your mind to be more optimistic.

In essence, seeing the funny side of situations turns drudgery into amusement.

Develop an eye for whimsy. See the silliness in human behavior. Listen with an appreciative ear. The world is brimming with fodder for laughter. The great comedian Steve Allen taught his protégés to practice having a funny state of mind by seeing comedy films, reading funny books, and hanging out with funny people as a daily diet.

Loosen up. Lighten up. You'll make better decisions and have far more capacity to deal with frustrations. And you just might enjoy living longer.

B. Detach

After you relax your body, then it's time to free up the mind by detaching from the controlling chatter in your brain. Cleaning out the clutter — worries about work, money troubles, rough relationships, and unresolved arguments — makes space for possibilities.

What are our weightiest thoughts?

Among those that confuse and control us the most are the judgments we form about situations in our world. As Stoic philosopher Epictetus said nearly 2,000 years ago, "Man is disturbed not by events that happen, but by his opinion of events that happen."

Of equal bearing are our concerns regarding the opinions others form about us. And yet, as acting coach Gary Austen insists, "It's none of your business what people think of you." It's your business to be in your body, giving 100% to the task at hand.

"For every moment you give to thinking about what someone else is thinking," Austen adds, "you are taking it from your best performance." Quit taking everything so personal and you open the space for a broader perspective and creative solutions.

Suzuki Roshi, author of Zen Mind, Beginners Mind, said, "In the beginners mind there are many possibilities. In the expert, there are few." Try to come from a place of "not already knowing the answer."

Quit trying to figure out what people are going to say before they stop talking. Quit making quick opinions about ideas.

Instead, be curious. In addition to seeing new ways to deal with challenges, people will find you much more interesting.

The paradox is that to control your mind you have to empty it.

You can see this rule at work when you participate in something just for the fun of it. When you have nothing to lose, you most likely do your best. You sink your longest putt, deliver a top-notch speech, find the win-win solution.

Why?

Because in eradicating past and future — fears, needs, judgments, and expectations — you're free to plunge into the present. This is where you'll see extraordinary results.

Olympic champion sprinter Michael Johnson says that although crossing the finish line feels great, the real thrill comes at the start of the race, when you're in the moment. That's when your mind, unconcerned about end results, competitors, or the passage of time, is focused on the experience itself. If there's nothing going on in your head to divert you, every fiber of your being is woven into the here and now. The challenge, Johnson says, is to maintain this presence until the experience is over and it's time to celebrate.

Once you are able to relax your body and detach from your thoughts, you'll see the present as a new world. When you are free of the need to be liked, appreciated and right, you'll see people in a new light. The spiritual therapist Byron Katie says, "The end of war is the beginning of intimacy."

Practice by consciously stopping your thoughts for one minute while observing the world around you. Tomorrow, increase your practice to two minutes. Each day, see how much longer you can go without judging. Then try doing this the next time you are upset. You'll see circumstances more clearly.

Here are four tips for helping you detach:

1. Focus on what you can control.

When you focus on what you can't control, like the work styles of others, the economy, and the way "things used to be," you have little energy left to create. Focus instead only on what you can control, like taking care of yourself, meeting the goals that excite you and discovering what you can delegate. This puts you in control. This makes you powerful.

2. Let go of what you thought would happen.

Clinging to your expectations blocks out possibilities. We all have pictures of what we thought a situation, conversation or meeting would look like. Then something else happened. If you aren't flexible, you will feel frustrated. Instead, choose to be present and go with the flow.

3. Walk lightly.

Taking your work seriously is admirable. Taking yourself seriously is not. Woody Allen said, "Comedy is tragedy plus time." Laughing today keeps you from wasting time.

4. Don't give up.

If you can't detach today, you may next time. You are teaching your old brain a new trick and it will take time.

C. Center

"Instincts never lie." "Trust your gut." "Listen to the voice deep inside you."

These are some of the many aphorisms that point to a well of wisdom and mindfulness beyond the bounds of the brain. According to many traditions, the true center of the mind lies in the center of the body. To get there, you move your awareness out of your head and into your core — an act known as centering.

Where is your core?

Some people say it's your heart. Others claim that the human core is more a feeling than a particular place. Performers and martial artists think of it as a central point just below the navel. Regardless of where your "center" lies, the point is to move your awareness into your body.

To find your central point, inhale deeply. Then move your attention to your heart or to the spot below your navel where the breath most fills your abdomen. While exhaling, keep your awareness on this spot. Let it settle there for a minute as you become familiar with this part of yourself.

With your awareness directed to this central point, scan your body to see what you can learn about your present state of being. Notice the feelings in your stomach. Do you detect hunger, discomfort, satiation? Pay attention to your legs. How do they feel? How about your toes? Check in with your fingers, your neck, and your hairline. Don't think. Just feel. Notice sensations arising everywhere, from the cuticles of your toenails to the hair follicles on your scalp. We rarely pay attention to our bodies until they cry out in pain. Begin today to create the habit of checking in. You'll not only know when you need to relax your body, you'll also be uniting your brain with your body, allowing your entire self to show up.

Sports psychologist Tom Kubistant, PhD, calls this activity "immersing." He asks golfers to move into themselves by releasing all thoughts, tensions and distractions, and to imagine themselves taking an elevator ride down from their brains into the interior of their bodies. Following his guidelines, golfers eventually settle into deeper levels of themselves, where their true talents lie.

Once you are comfortable keeping your awareness out of your head and at your center, add a variety of activities to your practice. Play sports, or try reading, listening to music, or hiking while centering in the moment for increasing periods of time. From this new perspective, you'll begin to see more details and hear finer nuances.

Now take centering to work with you, and into your social interactions. It will enhance your rapport with others. Whenever you are having difficulty staying present, place one hand lightly above your heart or your tummy and tap your fingers. This brings your attention out of your head and into your body. Feel your energy coming through your heart or center spot. Remind yourself to breathe.

As with all new habits, centering requires daily practice. Give yourself time to master it. The harder you try to center, the less effective your efforts will be. Start your practice in non-threatening situations. Stay persistent and consistent with daily sessions. Centering will become a habit instead of a technique.

D. Focus

The fourth step is to choose one thought to anchor yourself to as you maintain yourself in the present.

If you're like me, your thoughts have a way of sneaking into your brain no matter what you do. Therefore, if you have one thought to anchor on, keeping the others at bay, you can maintain ownership of your reactions.

I often focus on the outcome I want to achieve. Not the solution, but how I want myself, and others, to walk away feeling after an event or interaction. I think, "how do I want this story to end?"

For example, before a speaking engagement, I often write the word "fun" on a small piece of paper to set within my range of vision during the speech. If I'm committed to having fun, I know the audience too will enjoy themselves.

When speaking one-on-one, I'll often focus on the word "care" to help me remember that above all, I want people who work with me to feel that I care about them and value their ideas.

Focus is also important to maintain when working alone. To intensify your concentration on a complex project for a period of time each day, try focusing on how you want to feel when the work is done. If thinking out of the box is important, focus on the word "creativity." If accuracy is important, focus on the word "pride."

Whatever your objective might be, each extraneous thought that penetrates your brain is apt to decrease your effectiveness. When focussing is difficult remember to:

• *Attend to the Present*

Attending to the present moment takes courage and patience, especially while trying to overcome a lifetime of distracting mental habits. If patience has not been your forte, remind yourself that there are many aspects of life you have not yet seen. Keeping your attention anchored in the present will create within you a welcoming arena for new ideas and viewpoints.

Yes, you must trust that you will know what to do and say without thinking. This "standing in the unknowing" can be scary. It can also be magical. Not only will you see so much more, you'll also find that you are wiser and more capable than you ever imagined.

• *Approach Life with a Beginner's Mind*

I practice the following technique whenever I have difficulty staying in the moment. Practicing "beginner's mind" can help you shift into the present at will. How often do you put blinders on for purposes of being an expert, being right, or convincing yourself you know everything that's necessary? The better able you are to approach life with a beginner's mind, the more likely you will be to remove the last fragments of opinions and judgments that obstruct your view of possibilities in the moment.

I first learned of the Zen principle known as beginner's mind while working in Taiwan for a U.S. company. Simply, beginner's mind is the art of looking out on the world — people, places, and events — as if you've never seen them before. However, since everything in Asia was new to my senses, I couldn't put this practice to the test until I returned home.

Gloria, a Chinese colleague who had never been out of Taiwan, returned to the U.S. with me. It was mid-December, very late in the day. I was driving her from work to her hotel. I felt tired, hungry and resentful for being her chauffeur for two weeks. As we inched along through traffic, I complained about the number of tourists who converge in Arizona in winter, all choosing to drive at rush hour.

In the midst of my tirade, Gloria started to scream.

Much to my surprise, her face was radiant with delight. She pointed out the window. All I could see were houses.

Then it hit me — she was pointing at Christmas lights! She had never seen Christmas lights hung on houses.

I made a U-turn and headed for a street I knew where all the houses put up elaborate light displays. As Gloria excitedly took photographs to show off back home, I mentally viewed the scene through her eyes. Ever so briefly, I too could revel in seeing Christmas lights for the first time.

Pleased with this technique, I practiced beginner's mind for the next few days.

With fresh eyes, I relished in the graceful flight of a bird, the gentle opening of a flower, and the erratic jump of a grasshopper. Mastering this skill is easy, I decided, while looking at things I liked.

However, while observing people, places, and events I did not particularly like, the practice proved to be difficult, yet therein lay its magic.

My greatest lesson in practicing beginner's mind occurred with my cousin Stuart.

I didn't know Stuart well. He grew up in Cleveland, Ohio, far from my home in Phoenix. Although he seemed a nice enough guy, his whiny, slow-paced voice irritated me so much that I habitually ended our phone conversations as soon as I could.

A few years ago, the manufacturing company Stuart worked for transferred him to Douglas, Arizona. He called to tell me of the move and his promotion to plant manager. I congratulated him and said I'd visit someday. Given the five-hour drive from Phoenix to Douglas, I could graciously find excuses not to visit. Consequently, I missed his marriage to a woman he met in Mexico and the birth of his three children.

One day, Stuart called to say, "Marcia, I've been transferred to a plant outside of Phoenix. My family can't come for about three months. I'm all alone. Can we go to dinner?"

Guilt got the best of me. The following Tuesday evening, I sat in a Chinese restaurant across the table from my cousin Stuart. When he was midway into his fourth sentence, I thought, "Here is a real test of my ability to practice beginner's mind." I vowed to listen to Stuart as if I had never heard him before. To help me with my practice, I also decided to uncover something wonderful about him. Everyone has some hidden jewels of knowledge or experience, don't they? I vowed to find a gem in Stuart.

He talked. I listened. He droned on and on. My self-appointed mission grew more tedious as the minutes passed. Finally, the appearance of the waitress saved the day.

Yet before I could order, Stuart looked at her and said a few words in Chinese. I was impressed, until I saw the look of confusion on the waitress's face. I immediately began to wonder how long the evening would last.

Then Stuart said, "Oh, you don't speak Mandarin. You probably speak Cantonese."

He then spoke to her in Cantonese. This time, she smiled and replied.

Amazed, I said, "Stuart, I know you speak Spanish. And from my travels, I've learned that people who speak Mandarin rarely speak Cantonese. You must have studied quite a few languages in college."

He said, "Oh no, not in college. I run factories. People come from all over. I just listen and I pick it up."

I did indeed find something wonderful about Stuart.

At that point, his whine miraculously transformed into a singsongy cadence. Stuart, no longer a bore, turned into a fascinating person. I wanted to hear his stories. I found I enjoyed listening to cousin Stuart after all.

How many people have you blocked out of your life by erecting a wall of judgments and opinions? How many friends, coworkers, and relatives do you react to based on behavior they displayed months, if not years, ago? What foods or activities do you avoid because of unpleasant memories? What parts of your job do you dodge based on past disappointments? What parts of yourself do you circumvent? There is so much more to any person, place, and event than our minds typically allow us to see.

To enlarge your current perspective, remember that any time you observe a person, place, or event, you have two choices: you can either clear your mind and see with fresh eyes, or frame the picture in past perceptions. If you look through a filter of old judgments and opinions, you'll be stuck in the past. Instead, observe with a beginner's mind and revel in a world vibrant with possibility.

As radio commentator Paul Harvey says, here is the "rest of the story."

A year ago, toxic gas entered a house where Stuart was sleeping by himself. He died before the problem was discovered.

I went to the funeral. There I recognized family members I'd seen only in the photographs Stuart had shown me. Regretfully, I had never found the time to drive to Douglas to meet them.

Afterward, I went to his home, where I told the family about our night at the restaurant. They all laughed and thanked me for sharing the story. But before I could sit down, his mother said, "Let me tell you some other fabulous things about Stuart. Did you know he loved music? He wrote about a hundred folk songs. He even wrote three symphonies. All this, and he never took a music lesson in his life. He also loved poetry. He wrote lyrics for many of his songs. And did you know he changed his religion? I wasn't too happy about that…until the weekend I drove with him to visit a number of small-town congregations around Arizona. He loved to teach children his philosophy of love."

I promised my aunt that every opportunity I had, I would share my story about Stuart with others. It's not only a great lesson. It's also my way of honoring a great man I barely knew.

There's nothing more life-affirming than death. When we are faced with mortality, people matter. Little things count. While honoring the departed, we find goodness in life. We see clouds crawl across the sky and hear whispers of angels in the trees. This window stays open for a few days, then it silently closes as we go about our business.

Don't let illness and death be your only reminders of the magnificence of life. Don't let your brain batter your soul with judgments and opinions. Practice beginner's mind. See opportunities. Experience the pleasures of this planet. Savor the beauty in every soul you meet.

Gently hold your attention in the present. Sure, you're bound to feel pain and disappointment. Yet if you relax, detach, center, and approach life with a beginner's mind, something new and intriguing will appear just around the corner.

3. Emotional Identification

Earlier this year, I taught a few seminars at a chemical company in Texas. Between classes, I provided coaching for the managers to implement what they learned. After the first session, Larry, one of the managers, sent me an e-mail that he had received from a peer. It included a copy of the original e-mail Larry sent with comments from the other manager written in capital letters in red. Most of the comments started with the word, "WRONG."

Larry was clearly upset. He wanted me to agree with him that his colleague was rude and out to get him. Fortunately, before he sent back a scathing e-mail proving she was the one who was wrong, he called me.

I asked him, "Are you absolutely sure her only purpose in writing the e-mail was to prove you are an idiot?"

He reluctantly answered that there could be a possibility of something else on her mind.

I said, "If you didn't feel like she were trying to take away your credibility, what other reasons do you see for her behavior?"

He said he wasn't sure.

"Be creative," I suggested. "What do you think this letter is really telling you about her?"

Larry said, "Obviously, she is either mad at me or someone else. I guess we have to talk about what she is upset about, not whether who is right or wrong about when the report is due."

I was then able to coach Larry on how he could best approach this conversation with his colleague, starting with asking her if she were willing to find another way to handle disagreements with him since he wasn't comfortable with the e-mailed approach. After a difficult start, Larry told me, he found out that his colleague thought she was responsible for choosing the deadline dates, not him. She felt he was trying to undermine her authority. This led to a discussion on their roles and responsibilities. They agreed on some areas, and negotiated others. Working together, they found a better way to solve their problems.

From our coaching, I knew that the next time Larry received an e-mail with emotional overtones, he would be more inclined to look for the meaning between the words before reacting to the anger he felt. Larry was upset by the way the comments were made. Yet by looking below the surface issue, he found that his colleague was driven by her own emotional issues. A clash of reactions wouldn't help their working relationship. Instead, he opened himself to finding what was upsetting his colleague.

What does this take?

First, self-awareness so you can understand and clear your own clutter out of the way. And self-awareness helps you to develop the empathy for understanding what is at the source of the behavior in others. This takes stopping and standing in the present moment without acting on your first assumption or feelings.

Before we go on, let me explain that what you are about to read runs counter to some therapies and self-help books where behavioral change is based on changing thought patterns. "Change your thoughts, you change your behavior" is the prevailing belief. This technique may work well for some people in some situations. For the rest of us, in most situations where strong emotions are involved, we fail at teaching our brains new thought patterns. Although we can force different behaviors in the moment, few of us experience long-term change. Sometimes we get so discouraged we mentally beat ourselves up and worsen conditions.

What's missing?

Identifying the emotions that created the thoughts in the first place. It takes an awareness of the emotion to diffuse its power and then choose to act differently. The emotion may or may not disappear, but only then can we understand and change the thoughts that create the behavior.

How do we know that understanding the source of emotions can modify behavior? By looking at how the brain functions. If we study the neurobiology and the evolution of the brain, we see that input travels through the emotional centers first, the "primitive brain," activating bodily reactions before any data is sent to the logical portions. This flow acts to distort the data before our thinking brain even gets a hold of it, particularly if fear or anger is aroused.

This isn't an accident of nature. The design was first created when "eat or be eaten" and survival of the species were truly the priorities of the day. Above all, the brain is on the lookout for things that may harm us. The problem is our emotional brain doesn't differentiate a threat to the physical body from a threat to the ego. Therefore, if we sense the possibility of losing respect or not being valued for our ideas and actions, we tend to react as our ancestors did when faced with a physical threat. This response occurs before we even have a chance to assess the reality of the situation.

We can understand this more fully when we look at the evolution of the brain.

When creatures first arrived on the planet, the brain served them by functioning to regulate the body to keep it alive, and to alert the body when it needed to act in self-preservation.

Even now, all input still travels through this portion of the brain first. You can see this process in play whenever you are too hot, too cold or too hungry to do anything else. Concentrating is a difficult task. You have to take care of your needs first to protect your body.

Then the reptiles appeared on the planet. Their brains were larger and capable of thinking, but only of thought limited to discerning the answer to three questions. When faced with sensory input, the brain asked:

1. Can it hurt me? If the answer is no....
2. Can I eat it? If the answer is no...
3. Can I have sex with it?

The resulting behavior, in the words of Paul Pearsall in his book, *The Heart's Code,* was based on the four Fs — flight, fight, feast, or fornicate — generally in that order. The order is important in understanding our own behavior. Even though we may be much more civilized than the reptiles (although you may know some people you swear have reptile-like brains), our body still reacts to stimuli through this center first. Much of our behavior is based either on the fear of being hurt or the need to compete.

As mentioned earlier, the problem is that the primitive part of our brain reacts the same when someone looks as if they are going to hit us as when we perceive there is a possibility that someone we are with is going to hurt our feelings, test our authority or make us feel stupid. The body reacts in the same way as an animal sensing a threat, preparing us to flight or fight, releasing adrenaline, surging the blood flow to the big muscle groups, and directing thoughts toward protection.

Although we might have a more advanced, logical brain than the reptiles, our thoughts are distorted by this call for protection.

To complicate matters, the brain then evolved to include a broader array of emotions with the appearance of the mammals. The more advanced system allowed for feelings such as nurturing (mammals were the first to show affection to their young), jealousy, delight, loneliness, grief, anger and love. Mammals were the first to cry, the first to smile, and the first to kiss, which research now shows that all mammals do in their own ways.

Thus, we can add many Fs to the fight, flight feast, fornicate formula. Now we have family and favoritism, fastidiousness and fickleness, falsity and feistiness, fulfilled and fortunate, fantasy and philosophy (and a sense of fun).

Mammals can joke, lie, create dreams and regret dreams, all in one conversation.

As mammals evolved, they grew a new portion of the brain — the pre-frontal lobes — what we typically refer to as the "right and left brain." These lobes provide the functions of memory and learning, in addition to creativity and reasoning. Therefore, with the more highly-evolved mammals we see the inception of community, which in humans, led to the growth of cultures, civilization, the arts, religion and science.

With the ability to learn and remember, we also see the onset of neurosis and phobias, which are fear-based behaviors based on past experiences in addition to the present circumstances.

Therefore, the rational, thinking brain is also the irrational, remembering brain. We learn and we distort. The stronger the emotion felt, the greater the distortion.

The thinking brain also gave us the ability to suppress and rationalize as a means of protection because it's not always wise to fight or flee. Emotions are often stuffed in a blink of an eye, and present circumstances are seen through filters that talk us out of confronting the threat directly. And since we suppress, we are also passive-aggressive and manipulative or we misplace our aggression with irrational emotional outbursts when the suppressed anger overflows, such as seen in road rage or spousal abuse.

So the evolved human brain is also on the lookout for the enemy. The vigilance goes beyond physical harm to being alert to attacks on our respect and the loss of being liked, being heard and being acknowledged.

The first question the human brain asks is if what is present is a threat. The answer is based on the sum of our life experiences, so perceived threats grow in number as we age.

What does this all have to do with emotional intelligence? The key is to accept that any event can cause an emotional trigger in our brain — even if the reaction is relief or calm or satisfaction — and this emotion then sends messages to the rest of the brain and the body. If the emotion is negative, the reaction is often to suppress or rationalize.

The only way to outsmart the brain is to observe it and interrogate it, assessing if the input poses a real threat or not. You begin to see you have options instead of feeling as though you have no choice.

4. Choice

"I feel, therefore I think, therefore I am."

If you don't know what emotion you are acting on, you are not in control. The first challenge is to recognize the emotional reaction, then determine the source — what caused your brain to react — so you can consider possible actions to take.

Since the root of the word "intelligence" means "to make a choice between options," you are accessing your emotional intelligence when you perceive options. With this perception, you are free to choose.

You are in control, not your primitive brain.

I call the practice of determining the source of an emotion "peeling the onion" or delayering. You peel away the thoughts you have about a person or incident at the surface layer, the one that gives you a "good reason" for reacting with anger, vengeance, or surrender. You ask yourself, "What am I afraid of losing?" or "What do I feel has been taken away from me (such as control, being right, being liked or appreciated)?" Then you can ask if the fear or the loss is valid.

At that moment, you can see you have choices. You may choose to stay with your emotions. You may choose to take time out to process them and return later to ask for what you need when feeling more neutral or more powerful. You may choose to breathe deeply and let the emotion go, sometimes even laughing at your primitive brain.

In my last job, I spent three weeks researching and writing a proposal for building a learning center. The proposal included a large budget. I set a meeting to present this proposal to the CEO.

The day before my presentation, I dropped by my manager's office to show him my work. He quickly flipped through the proposal, stopping on the last page. "You can't ask for that," he said pointing at a line item in the budget.

How do you think I responded?

I jumped into the battle, intent on proving him wrong. At one point, I think I knew he was right, but what do you think I was protecting? Of course, my ego. I didn't stop by his office to get his critique. I was searching for a compliment.

Finally, he demanded I change the budget before seeing the CEO. I grabbed the proposal in disgust. Then something clicked in my head... the real reason for my anger. I said, "Time out. You may be right. But what I really wanted was for you to acknowledge the effort I put into this project."

He answered, "What are you talking about? You always do good work. Change that one item and you have a masterpiece."

"I need to hear you tell me that once in a while."

"All right," he reluctantly said. As I turned to go, he added, "But you never tell me when I do a good job."

I was stunned. He was right. Stuck in my own need for appreciation, I couldn't see that he had the same need as I. I forgot that I had to manage up as well as down.

Since I had the presence of mind to go beyond the surface issue and ask for what I really needed, we were able to improve our relationship. Even better, I began watching him more closely.

Using my curious eye, I found that he never read anybody's reports. In fact, it didn't appear that the man liked to read. Then I noticed that he transposed words in his sentences, and often struggled with the order of letters in a word. For instance, he couldn't say "permanent," saying "pernament" instead. It then dawned on me that my boss was probably dyslexic. I imagined he had spent years learning how to hide his disability, and had succeeded in spite of it. From that day on, I never gave him a report to read if I could instead read it to him or just highlight the contents.

This incident taught me the power of knowing what is causing my emotional reaction, then making the request for what I need to resolve the situation.

Do you choose compassion over intolerance? Love over jealousy? Intimacy over fear? Courage over complacency? Curiosity over impatience?

When you don't agree with someone or you are working toward a solution with a group, how do you want others to perceive you? How do you want your story to end? Is it more important to stick to your story, to demand others play by your rules? Or can you choose to reframe the situation and consider new possibilities?

The STIR It Up technique is designed to assist you in getting to the source of your emotions to help you find new possibilities for actions and results. The steps to this technique can be found in Appendix C.

■ Making Your Own Movie

Awareness is the capacity to stand apart from ourselves and examine our thinking, our intentions, our behaviors and our effects on what is around us. As we learn to recognize and accept our relationship to

*the large and complex world, we accept more and more responsibility
for the consequences of our actions, and even of our thoughts.*

— *The Emotional Intelligence Activity Book,*
published by Six Seconds, Inc.

In other words, if you could at any moment, stop and watch yourself in a movie, hearing your mental dialogue as well as observing your behavior, what would you see? Often you would witness a wonderful comedy. It could be said that emotional intelligence is measured by how quickly you can laugh at yourself. At least, you might change your mind more often.

CHAPTER 4

■

RELATING AND
INFLUENCING

As you increase your self-awareness, you'll find an increase in your empathy. The clarity you develop when observing your own reactions offers insights into the sources of behavior in others. From this new understanding of what triggers reactions, you may find new ways of relating to and influencing those you work with.

Therefore, when it comes to dealing with those who are most difficult — who react by complaining, blaming, competing, blindly striving for perfection, slapping down with arrogance or sabotaging with complacency — instead of reacting to their behavior, you might find a different way to respond. As a result, you will at least decrease your stress if not find better solutions and improve your relationships.

In fact, once we take charge of our emotional reactions and can stand more solidly in the present moment, other people's needs and their emotional triggers become almost transparent. We all want the same things — to be acknowledged, cared about, and respected. No matter how insensitive a person may seem, few people on this planet set out to hurt someone else. Rudeness, misunderstandings and impropriety often happen in the course of grasping for the attention, control and appreciation we need, not because we want to hurt.

Take these statements as examples: "It's not my job." "That will never work here." "I don't have time to do that presentation." Often we find fear at the root of these statements, not laziness, haughtiness or apathy. The trick is to not take these statements as personal affronts. Most people are not looking to pick a fight. They are seeking to protect themselves. Even an act of vengeance has either fear or anger triggered by a perceived loss at the source of the action.

It's true that some people put forth a challenge to see "what stuff you're made of." Yet even in these cases, their actions aren't motivated by the desire to make you look stupid. They are either trying to help you step up to the plate, or trying to eradicate their own feelings of inadequacy by proving they are better than you. If they are trying to help you reach higher, then they truly honor your talent. If they are using you to build themselves up, then recognize that they must think you are worthy of being a benchmark.

It's your choice whether to feel disrespected or not. If you feel you are right, acknowledge that there are many ways to view a situation, with two of those viewpoints in the room. If you feel you were tricked, then thank the person for choosing you as a worthy straight man (or punching bag, whichever is more relevant). If the person says something really off-the-wall, consider asking if you can quote your adversary in your next book or magazine article (they might think twice about what they say to you next time).

The key to using emotional intelligence with others is the same as using it for yourself — become an objective observer. Then you can begin to see a range of possible answers to the following questions:

— What is driving them to act that way?
— What is their brain protecting?
— Are they afraid of not being heard, of not being acknowledged, of being made wrong, or of failing?
— Do they feel I've disrespected them or devalued their ideas?
— Did they have an expectation that I failed to fulfill?
— Do I intimidate them, and are they afraid I won't approve or like them?
— Are they concerned that others won't find their ideas/work credible or worthy of respect?
— Have I created a safe space so they can speak their mind? Do I *want* them to feel safe enough to speak their mind?

You may be able to answer these questions on your own. Or you may have to ask the person to find out. Yet, before you even begin the conversation, you have to determine if you are able to speak neutrally.

How are you feeling? Can you talk to them in such a way that they would welcome the opportunity to discover possible options of how to be together? You may need to take a deep breath, stop your own mental chatter, then focus on the outcome and ask yourself, "What ending do you want this story to have?"

I've found that three conditions must be present in our own mind-set before we are able to engage others in the exploration of emotional sources of conflict and possible solutions:

1. willingness,
2. desire, and
3. courage.

If you are willing to do what it takes to create a win-win scenario with someone and you have the courage to say what you perceive, then you can relax, detach, center and focus on listening with a clear mind.

Once you are aware of what is at the core of a person's behavior, you will be able to determine the best course of action to create the outcome you desire.

1. Willingness

An old riddle asks, "If three frogs are sitting on a lily pad and one decides to jump, how many frogs are left behind?" The answer is three, because deciding to jump is not the same as jumping. Here is another riddle: "If three people are sitting on a couch griping about their co-worker's lack of commitment to a project and one decides it's time to address the problem, how many people are left sitting on the couch?" Once again, the answer is three. Before movement toward a solution can take place, it takes:

1. The willingness to accept evidence that my assumptions about someone/the situation may not be true AND
2. The willingness to work on finding a solution together.

So what does it take to be willing?

Unfortunately, it often takes a crisis or feeling discouraged before we are willing to see a situation or person in a new light. We see the difficulties we have connecting with others, or we sense a lack of buy-in to our ideas, yet say nothing to improve the situation. In fact, if we do not choose to change these circumstances, we end up helpless witnesses to the difficulties created by the inaction.

In other words, if you want appreciation for your ideas from your manager or peers, you should ask for the acknowledgment BEFORE getting angry and combative. If you want a better working relationship with someone, you should arrange for a personal meeting BEFORE further damage is done. If you feel overwhelmed, you should seek help BEFORE making a big mistake. Be aware of your own fears of rejection, looking wrong, or feeling stupid. Then ask yourself if your fears are valid. If you aren't sure, be willing to take the leap to change your circumstances for the better.

What blocks willingness?

Most obstructions are blamed on the lack of time or money. In reality, inaction more frequently comes from a refusal to face our fears. Iyanla Vanzant, in her book *One Day My Soul Just Opened Up*, writes, "I was not willing to make people angry or hurt their feelings... I was not willing to sound weird or stupid or like a know-it-all. I was not willing to run the risk of being wrong. I was not willing or prepared to defend myself if I were challenged... I knew what needed to be done, but I was not willing to do it."

Such fears hold us captive, yet acknowledging them diffuses their power. Fear of disapproval can be vanquished as soon as we understand that other people will not always be happy with what we do or say. Indeed, some will *never* like what we do or say. Fear of making a mistake is surmountable when we admit that we are all less than perfect. In fact, sometimes just declaring a fear out loud takes the air out of the emotion.

When I admit that I'm envious of someone, afraid that I'll never reach the same level of success as they, I can laugh at the silliness of my fear. And I can admit that my envy has nothing to do with how much I respect the person regardless of my jealousy. In fact, most of my fears lose control over me once I admit them out loud. Then I'm free to do what is in my best interest.

When it comes to making decisions for ourselves, we would do well to befriend someone who will support our willingness. The greater the discomfort, the more vital the role of at least one person to listen to us and cheer us on.

Be careful of your well-thought-out excuses. Yes, you have loved ones who need your paycheck. You would rather not offend your boss. You have too much to do than to sit down and have a "heart-to-heart" talk with a colleague that could result in a waste of time. Yet in truth, you don't have the time to let the poison in your relationships course deeper. You don't have enough capacity to suppress all your negative emotions without affecting your health and your ability to be happy. And you don't have enough margin in your bottom line to let problems in morale and commitment erode productivity.

Try the Exercise in Willingness on page 46.

From the Willingness Exercise, you may learn two things:

1. In practice, being willing to see options is difficult when we spend all our time fortifying the walls in which we live.
2. We put a lot of energy holding on to ideas that make no difference in the big scheme of things.

Willingness is essential to resolving problems and growing relationships. Can you step out of your frame, out of "the world according to you," for the chance of improving communications and results? If you do, you might find no good reason to change your mind. Or, you might find many.

In essence, willingness is the ability to let go of what you believe and try on new ideas and actions without knowing the outcome. It's performing without knowing if the presentation will elicit applause. It's speaking without knowing if anyone cares to listen. It's listening without knowing how people will judge your silence. It's showing you care without knowing if your efforts will be rebuffed. Sometimes you won't get all you had hope for. But isn't it worth the attempt? Woody Allen said that once we master Oneness, then we have Twoness to deal with. Can you boldly venture into this new frontier?

2. Desire

The second element in the formula for relational success is "desire." I may be willing to work on new solutions, but my desire is not strong enough for my willingness to persist in the face of obstacles. The distinction between willingness and desire is subtle, but different enough to block action.

In other words, talk is cheap. You have to find a way "to want it to happen" before you are capable of permanent results. Wanting is an emotion. You have to find the reasons for mustering your desire since they aren't always apparent. Without heart-felt desire, it's easier to acquiesce to circumstances than to take responsibility for results.

Children see the world around them as responsible for their upsets. Troubled teenagers blame their parents, teachers and others for the injustices they experience. Most of us adults, although intellectually aware that we are responsible for our own lives, tend to subscribe to this belief only when things are going well. We prefer to attribute our unhappiness to the company, to our dysfunctional upbringing or to our children, spouses and friends. We wallow in gloom as if we have earned the right to be miserable. "The ingenuity of self-deception is inexhaustible," wrote essayist Hannah Moore in 1881.

Ultimately, to create desire, we need to accept that we have chosen

Exercise in Willingness

You will need a pen, paper, and a timer.
You can do this alone or with a partner.

1. List three beliefs that are important to you but don't make a big difference in the world.

For example, does it bug you when people put the toilet paper roll on the wrong way? Do the dishes have to be washed immediately or can they sit in the sink? Should people return what they borrow to the place that they found it? Should clothing be folded a certain way? Is being on time always important? Should the toilet seat be up or down? Should a thorough analysis of options be made before any large purchase? Come up with three of your own pet peeves. Just make sure they are a small in the big scheme of things.

2. Pick one belief.

Set your timer to go off in one minute. As quickly as you can, spend the next 60 seconds finding all the reasons why this one belief may not be true. Argue against yourself. Be creative, even silly. You can have your belief back in 60 seconds. If you have a partner, have your partner argue for your belief while you argue against it. This is more difficult and more effective.

3. Ask yourself these questions.

What did you learn about being attached to your belief? How hard was it to let go? If the exercise was difficult, repeat steps 1–3 again with another belief from your list.

4. Apply what you learned in the exercise to the workplace.

Imagine working on a project where you have a belief about how it should be done differently than the way it is being handled. Are you able to get out of your belief about how it should be done? Now picture this as it applies to changing priorities in the workplace, or changing processes. If you have been complaining about or fearful of the changes, can you find good reasons to accept the dictates you've been given?

Answer these questions:

Where do your beliefs have you trapped at work? Where have you become so attached to your way of doing something that you cannot imagine any other way of handling a situation or dealing with a person? Can you argue against yourself, breaking your paradigms to allow for change and growth?

Once you begin to loosen your own blocks, you will begin to recognize when other people are so attached to their beliefs that they are blinded to possibilities.

What can you do to help them see options?

Try playing the game with others, using it as a technique to inspire creativity and brainstorm alternative solutions. Always acknowledge someone else's perspective first as valid, then ask if they are willing to see the situation from a different angle. Remember, they can't feel as if you are taking away their control or that you are making them wrong. Make them right, then see if you can help them to perceive more than one right answer.

our difficult situations. In accepting ourselves as agents, we remove the veil of self-deception and give voice to our heart's desires. What would your life look like if you were in control? How free would you feel if you felt you lived by choice? How badly do you want this for yourself?

If we can inspire our desire, we become creators instead of victims. Even choosing to do nothing for a period of time for a specific reason is more powerful than waiting for others to take action.

In short, to be effective we must desire to improve our situation. Rather than view a personal hardship as someone else's responsibility, we claim accountability for it, commit ourselves to positive growth, and exercise the power we have to shape our reality.

How do you want your stories to end? Vision yourself as powerful and growing daily. Troubles seem smaller when we hitch ourselves to something bigger than the dramas that play out in front of us day-to-day. Let go of expectations of what you thought things "should" look like. Even if options don't become apparent right away, you're bound to feel less stress in the release. With desire, we ride from misery to joy.

To assess your desire, follow these steps:

1. *Hesitate.* Instead of acting on your first impulse, before you blow someone off, resist advice, give advice before it's asked for, say nothing in order to let things work out on their own, demand action without seeking the source of inaction, make a promise you're not sure you can keep or say no without thinking it through...

   take a deep breath.

2. *Assess* your motivation. Ask yourself, "Why do I want to do this? If I act this way, will I like the outcome?" If you aren't sure, try to vision yourself carrying out your first impulse. Does it make you feel good, really? If yes, will I still feel good about my actions tomorrow, next week, next year? If no to either question...

3. *Discover.* How would you like to feel in the end? How do you want others to see you? Who do you want to be? Seek to find the answers that will allow your heart to dance with you in the process. These answers become your roots as the storms come in. Desire must be present for personal growth. Too many failures happen due to the words, "My heart wasn't in it." What

will it take for you to feel a commitment, even a passion, for taking the actions that will yield the best results?

3. Courage

What will it take for you to be a courageous leader?

One of the reasons I became a personal coach was to be able to work with people over time to help them bring their visions into reality. As a trainer, I saw thousands of people leave my classes ready to try out their new skills and ideas. Yet the enthusiasm rarely lasted for more than a day. Once faced with a conflict that pushed their buttons or a task they preferred not to do, the good intentions flew out the window. Yes, they were willing to try new techniques...to a degree. Yes, they desired better results...to a point. As soon as the negative emotion rushed in, they lost the gumption to practice behaviors they weren't yet comfortable with. No way would they tell their boss the truth. No way would they confront the team with their observations. No way would they admit that they were wrong.

The protective brain once again silenced the heart.

It takes courage to change your mind. It takes bravery to say what is on your mind when you're not sure it will be well received. Yet continuing to say "no" to possibilities stops progress dead in its tracks. Rationalizing and defending behavior keeps us nestled in a safe, mediocre and suffocating world. Saying, "Yes, there are possibilities!" is the greatest gift you can offer yourself.

Improvisational actors are taught to say "yes" in order to keep a scene moving. Whatever it takes — deep relaxation or sheer will — they are expected to go with the flow and engage in the motion around them. So it is in life, the ultimate improvisational stage. The trick is to step into the moment with both feet.

Therefore, relational success requires you muster the courage to act with or without a clear picture of the outcome. If you say, "I desire to improve the situation, but just not today," then you'll probably miss your chance. Someone else will take the job, create the product, write the story, trademark the business name, or discover what you've been thinking all along.

What gives rise to the courage to act? Mythologist Joseph Campbell advised us to discover the meaning of courage by looking at what makes a person a "hero."

The journey all heroes take, he said, leads them on mysterious adventures and into fabulous battles, bringing them home with knowledge and rewards to share. Heroes call on their internal powers to stand strong before monsters. They clear their minds, casting out the urge to resist, fight or flee. In the clearing, they access their greatest weapon — instinctual consciousness, or wisdom.

Courage, in this sense, is the thread that weaves willingness and desire into the structure of who we are. It promotes a feeling of wholeness, integrating aspects of ourselves that have been contrary to our nature, transforming us as we take on the trials of life.

Therefore, whenever you choose to do something when your mind is saying, "no," you are acting as a hero. You are facing your fear and choosing to do what you feel from your heart is right. This requires you relax, detach, center and focus on 1) the outcome you want to create, 2) how you want to feel when you walk away from the situation and 3) what you believe can happen if everyone took the higher road. Standing strong in the present moment allows us to go into our hearts and listen for answers. "As a man thinketh in his heart, so he is," the Bible tells us. Experience teaches us that the more accustomed we are to taking risks, the more adept we are at bouncing back.

Sometimes I take a deep breath, clear my mind, tap my heart and focus on my vision while scheduling threatening events into my daily calendar. Then when it comes time to act, I punch in the phone number, make the major purchase, take the day off, get a commitment to meet for that much-needed conversation, start my next book, throw out my old books or take the first step in the next chapter of my life.

When you practice courage and are true to your values and desires and things don't work out, you know that you gave it your best shot. Know this, then when you can, go to a quiet place where you can hear the whispers of your grandest dreams. As the Buddha put it, "To be happy, rest like a great tree in the midst of it all."

The moment the mind is empty, joy finds a way to shine through. Using this light, declare your willingness, claim your desires and boldly leap over the puddles the rain left behind.

■ INFLUENCE

In addition to seeing choices and taking risks, you can access your emotional intelligence to hear the desires and needs of those you work with. More than ever, we need to create cultures of respect and dignity.

When it comes to staying with an organization, either physically or mentally, people need to feel as if they are valued for their intelligence and ability.

This acknowledgment may look different for each person. According to Paul Pearsall in *The Heart's Code*, managers need to become intimate allies with their employees. Only then can managers determine how each person who works for them can be helped to feel worthwhile.

It is critical that we notice emotional triggers in others and attempt to understand them to determine how we can influence others to see and act in a different way. We need to notice reactions in faces, bodies and words, to pay attention to them as we are deciding what to say and how to act.

Instead of pushing your point, acknowledge when someone is tense or uncomfortable. Instead of accepting words of agreement, probe deeper when the words don't match the pursed lips, lack of eye contact or clenched fist. Instead of backing down when someone says they would rather not talk, sense what they really need from you, be it attention, appreciation or love. Then see what you can offer that might open the door to further communication.

Of course, this requires we continue to be alert to our own emotional triggers. Once they appear, how quickly can we choose to either ask for what we need or to release the hold the trigger has on our thoughts? The quicker we choose, the sooner we clear the space to be with others 100 percent.

One of the main reasons for striving to be emotionally intelligent is to be able to create desirable outcomes in our communications with others. Too often, we get stuck in an emotional reaction because a situation or person does not conform to our view of how the world should be. In order to get beyond this position, we must be able to go beyond the boundaries of our perceptions to see another way.

When we are able to see the event from another angle and the person in a different light, we can also see new possibilities for solutions. There's the possibility we'll even see ways of helping others to accept alternative ideas.

For example, a former marine attended one of my keynote speeches and challenged me to see that fear can be a great motivator and character builder.

Instead of disagreeing with him, I acknowledged his point of view. Fear can be a great motivator. Then I said, "We need your type of leadership when working with people in times of crisis. And I'm hoping we don't see the need for creating war zones at work. Few people I know could handle this type of motivation for more than 10 years without burning out."

Other people in the audience piped in with research about how today's workforce is not responding to scare-tactics as they did in prior years.

The man agreed, and thanked me for helping him understand more clearly what I was talking about. I didn't give him earth-shattering news, but I acknowledged that his beliefs were important to his identity. My beliefs may have threatened him. Yet, as long as I acknowledged him first, he was able to open up to me. If I had not, my stage would have become his war zone.

In the end, we both came to a greater understanding of each other and the power of emotional intelligence.

Thus, the question is not, "How can I get them to see?" but instead, "How do I want them to feel?" To get satisfactory results when faced with a conflict, the primary consideration must be emotional. Parties should leave the table feeling heard and valued, regardless of the outcome.

Generally, if you get people to see your way with force, they may "see" briefly, then go away looking for reasons to make you wrong. Even if they concede to your point of view, there may be irreparable damage to the relationship. We "see" and go away calling the person who made us wrong a "jerk" or an "idiot," regardless of how smart the person may be.

Respect is built on force only in times of crisis. At all other times, it is built on a genuine demonstration of how much we honor the person we are speaking to as an intelligent being, even if we disagree with them.

Would you rather win as a jerk or find the win-win as a sage? Focus on connecting instead of proving and you're more likely to find ways to influence.

What does it take to be able to make this connection? The willingness to listen to ideas contrary to yours, the desire to create an outcome that works for everyone, even if it means you may have to shift your opinions and ideas, and the courage to jump into the unknown.

Willingness + Desire + Courage = Creativity, the ability to see options, to rise above your reactional brain to be present to all the possibilities before you in the moment.

When you step off your own position, you can see what is at the source of an emotional reaction in others. Here are some common behaviors seen at work:

— A need for approval or acceptance can cause a person to either refuse to take risks or to take too many risks. It also shows up with people who either stick to doing what is comfortable or never say no to anyone, promising too much. Looking closely, you will see that their actions are designed to either ward off criticism or to attract positive attention. Unmet, these needs can lead to a restrained rage. It may take only a little acknowledgment, trust and guidance to help these people feel more confident with their work.

— A need to feel important, appreciated and held in esteem can drive people not only to overwork but to demand perfection from others. They may be hypersensitive to criticism, and constantly judge their work performance against that of others, looking to stay "one up" so they don't feel inadequate. They show arrogance as opposed to confidence. Although it's difficult to compliment these people, finding ways to acknowledge their work without comparing them to others is one way to help them "get over themselves." Check your own emotional reactions when in conversation with these people so you can recognize the chance to shift their perspective when it shows up.

— A need for prosperity often drives someone to have an exaggerated desire to make money, have possessions and be promoted. This need made it difficult for me to teach management skills in Taiwan. Their drive to have what the Americans have was their strongest motivation. The difficulty with this mindset is that there is never enough money and titles to go around to satisfy everyone. Whenever possible, management needs to create cultures where other means of motivation are valued and provided.

— The need for achievement drives people to see immediate results, which drives the slower, more accurate workers crazy. Break work into smaller tasks so people can feel a sense of achievement sooner.

— The need to control, to be right and to win are active when people do everything possible to avoid being seen as vulnerable, weak, worthless, stupid or incompetent. The thought of letting anyone see their all-too-human flaws is unbearable. Here, your best defense is to gracefully and honestly acknowledge the need you think is at the source of the person's reactions, then make a direct request. For example, if you say, "I see that you would like to control this project. Although I know you've had experience on similar projects, I want to make sure everyone is heard. Sometimes a fresh perspective is just as useful. Will you support the team by letting everyone have a chance to speak?" Or, if someone has a need to be right and corrected you in front of others, you might say, "I know that accuracy is important to you. I apologize for the oversight. In the future, I'd like to discuss situations like this in private instead of in public. Would that be possible?" Don't be afraid to set boundaries. The loss of your self-esteem is a far greater cost than the consequence of someone not liking your request.

— The need for harmony, on the other hand, can keep people from standing up for themselves when they are right or when they should take charge of a situation. Wounds fester and problems multiply as they try to smooth things over. To get the best results, draw the individual out, helping him or her to speak up.

— The need for consistency can be seen in those who complain about change, no matter how inevitable or beneficial it may be. Help these people see that the personal consequences of the change are not drastic, then go slowly, allowing them time to adjust. Another technique for dealing with complaints about change is to ask the person, "What is your request?" This helps them to think of what action they would like to see take place instead of obsessing on what circumstances they don't like. If the request is unreasonable, acknowledge the answer, then say, "Okay, what else?" Eventually, they will get the point.

Need-based behaviors often take the fun out of work and injure our relationships. Needs can have a positive effect as well, helping us achieve desired results. Taking control can be useful when there is a need to jumpstart a stalled project. Instilling harmony can help a team overcome conflict. Practicing consistency keeps daily tasks on track.

The key is to identify when actions are beneficial or detrimental. If the behavior isn't appropriate for the situation, then ask for what you would like to see instead.

It's also helpful if you model the behavior you want. In other words, if you catch yourself reacting inappropriately to a situation based on your own need to control, to be right, to be heard or to stay safe, admit that your need got the best of you, then change your behavior. Modeling self-awareness, vulnerability and flexibility are signs of leadership no matter what position you hold.

I had a friend tell me that my rigid, insensitive boss was, "doing his best with the amount of light he had."

This made sense to me.

Then she said, "Your light is so big while his is so little, it is your responsibility to model what big light looks like."

Reluctantly, I took on the challenge.

She was right. Over time, the relationship with my boss improved.

Also, remember to keep up your self-care. The ability to resolve conflicts and work together well with others is hindered by sleep deprivation, poor nutrition, noise pollution, personal problems, lack of money and a shortage of friends. Your mental house must be clean before you entertain guests.

■ THE EMPEROR'S NEW CLOTHES

Remember the children's story about the emperor's new clothes? The emperor was told his invisible clothes were the most regal robes on the planet. He couldn't see the clothes, but agreed, not wanting to look stupid. And although he did look stupid parading around naked, no one would tell the emperor for fear of being killed.

Whether or not you believe that focusing on the emotional aspects of communications is useful or not, know that if you pretend these emotions don't exist, you will appear as the gullible emperor. No matter how good you might think you are at hiding your emotions, they affect your communications and ability to connect.

Don't you sense when someone else feels strong emotions? You may ignore your intuition, but the tiny voice still speaks to you. Have you ever walked into a room and felt the air was thick with conflict? You probably felt an urge to be somewhere else unless engaging in conflict is your pleasure. So even if you don't want to talk about the emotional energy you detect, why neglect the information you are receiving? If you do, you are throwing out important information that could help you make better decisions.

And don't think you're helping others by hiding your emotions. In fact, when we "stonewall," we create the experience of "talking to a blank wall," which creates more anger and frustration in our relationships. We are influenced by the temperamental tone people project.

One negative emotion can arouse the protective brain in another, thus poisoning a conversation.

As soon as you can, discover and admit to the source of your emotions. Perhaps then you can work with them to find a better way to live and work together. Yes, there are times when speaking your mind could be a bad choice, but if you clear your mind and center in the present moment, you're likely to determine when is the best time to speak up.

Remember that the brain's primary function is to protect. The heart's is to connect. This means that often, the brain and heart compete with one another, making decisions difficult. It is our primitive brain system that takes up most of our cerebral time by worrying, plotting, and defending, overpowering the choices preferred by the heart. Rational thinking becomes rationalizing and defending, fighting and hiding. Chronic emotional reactions to minor stresses result in suppressed hostility, impatience, frustration and exhaustion. Connecting, loving and caring only happen when deemed completely safe even though these feeling are what we need to heal our stress.

"We are living with a B.C. brain in A.D. time," someone wise once said.

Of course, we need our protective, rational brain to survive and prosper. The goal is to honor all the messages we receive. While the brain helps us to navigate through life, the heart allows us to find humor, gratitude, enlightenment and meaning in the darkest of moments. It's time we realigned all our intelligences to make the best choices for ourselves.

Remember, relax your body, detach from controlling thoughts and needs, center yourself in the present moment, then focus on "who" you want to be seen as when with others and "how you want your stories to end."

Laugh at yourself as often as you can. Celebrate the good since there is always something to affect our best-laid plans. To be human is to create, to frolic, to love and to be alive.

When we bring our heart to work, we allow ourselves and those around us to experience all that life can offer at any given moment. Who would not follow a leader who keeps the heart in mind?

The challenge is to create emotionally intelligent cultures in our organizations. Leaders who orchestrate this transformation will have a competitive advantage in the years to come.

APPENDIX A

TAKING STOCK OF YOUR EMOTIONS: AN INVENTORY OF FEELINGS TO INCREASE YOUR EMOTIONAL DISCERNMENT AND COMPREHENSION

"Emotions" refers to the mental and physiological states characterized as feelings. It's often difficult to put a name on what you're experiencing because it's likely that your brain is processing more than one reaction to your circumstances at a time. Not only do feelings overlap and blend, but there are hundreds of emotions, each with many gradations of intensity, that make emotional awareness a difficult skill to master. Yet the more adept you are at discerning the force that is shaping your mood and mental status, the greater will be your ability to manage your behavior. You can choose to act in the moment based on possibilities instead of reacting to the moment based on habit. In other words, you respond with intelligence instead of impulse. The result is greater effectiveness, productivity and confidence. And, as you come to comprehend your own emotions and behavior, you increase your understanding for what drives the actions of those around you. With this knowledge, you can improve your relationships, and above all, your happiness. Emotional intelligence is a key factor to enhancing your quality of life.

For the next two weeks, carry a watch or travel alarm with you. At the times listed on the schedule, fill in the blanks with 1) what you are doing, generically, and who you are doing it with (working alone, talking with family, attending a meeting, leading a meeting, driving, eating with a friend, reading alone, etc.) and 2) the emotion(s) you are feeling in the moment. Use the inventory on page 59 to help you identify what you are feeling. If you are sleeping during the times listed, adjust the hours on the assessment to fit your schedule. The exact times are not essential. It's more important to begin to recognize emotional patterns, and to determine what circumstances elicit specific responses. However, it's important to assess what you are feeling *in the moment* instead of relying on memory. Emotional intelligence is the art of identifying your feelings at the time they occur so you can better understand behavior and learn how to rationally choose your reactions.

Remember, you are seeking to understand your feelings. You are not trying to change them. They are not right or wrong. Therefore, honesty is important. However, recognition alone can often diffuse or increase an emotional reaction. You may find that over time, the intensity of some moods decrease, while other sensations, hopefully the more pleasant ones, increase. That's why emotional intelligence helps in all aspects of your personal growth.

FEELINGS INVENTORY

Related to:

Anger
Fury
Outrage
Hatred
Resentful
Exasperated
Annoyed
Irritated
Vengeful
Cheated
Belligerent
Rebellious
Resistant
Envious
Superior
Defiant
Contempt
Repulsed
Appalled
Offended
Distrustful
Cynical
Wary
Concerned
Apprehensive

Fear
Nervous
Dreading
Worried
Afraid
Anxious
Edgy
Restless
Frightened
Threatened
Stressed
Obsessed
Overwhelmed

Disheartened
Baffled
Confused
Lost
Disoriented

Disconnected
Trapped
Lonely
Isolated
Sad
Grieving
Dejected
Gloomy
Desperate
Depressed
Devastated
Helpless
Weak
Vulnerable
Moody
Serious
Somber
Disappointed
Hurt
Defective
Shy
Unloved
Abandoned
Frail
Queasy
Weary
Tired
Burned-Out
Apathetic
Complacent
Bored
Brainless
Exhausted
Frustrated
Grumpy
Impatient
Testy
Wound-Up

Shame
Humiliated
Mortified
Embarrassed
Ashamed
Uncomfort-
able
Guilty

Regretful
Remorseful
Reflective
Sorrowful
Detached
Aloof

Surprise
Shocked
Startled
Stunned
Amazed
Astonished
Impressed

Impassioned
Enthusiastic
Excited
Aroused
Delirious
Passionate
Crazed
Euphoric
Thrilled
Competitive
Willful
Determined
Confident
Bold
Eager
Optimistic
Gratified
Proud
Gushy

Happy
Joyful
Blissful
Amused
Delighted
Triumphant
Lucky
Pleased
Silly
Dreamy
Enchanted
Appreciative

Grateful
Hopeful
Intrigued
Interested
Engrossed
Alive
Vivacious

Calm
Contented
Relieved
Peaceful
Relaxed
Satisfied
Reserved
Comfortable
Receptive
Forgiving
Accepting
Loved
Serene

Regard
Adoration
Admiration
Reverent
Loving
Affectionate
Secure
Respectful
Friendly
Sympathetic
Compassion
Tenderness
Generous

Other:
(Write in
Your Own)

EMOTIONAL ASSESSMENTS

Week 1	Mon.	Tues.	Wed.	Thu.	Fri.	Sat.	Sun.
7:30 am							
Doing							
Feeling							
11:00 am							
Doing							
Feeling							
3:00 pm							
Doing							
Feeling							
9:00 pm							
Doing							
Feeling							

EMOTIONAL ASSESSMENTS

Week 2	Mon.	Tues.	Wed.	Thu.	Fri.	Sat.	Sun.
7:30 am							
Doing							
Feeling							
11:00 am							
Doing							
Feeling							
3:00 pm							
Doing							
Feeling							
9:00 pm							
Doing							
Feeling							

APPENDIX B

SELF-CARE CHECKLIST

■ ENVIRONMENT

- ☐ Is your office organized so you can find things easily?
- ☐ Are your workspaces pile-free?
- ☐ Does your home provide you comfort and a peaceful place where you can think?
- ☐ Are your appliances in working order?
- ☐ Do you have back-up systems in case of electric failure? Computer crashes?
- ☐ Do you maintain your car regularly and is everything working properly?
- ☐ Does your home have a smoke detector, fire extinguisher and easy contact to the police?
- ☐ Do you keep enough home and office supplies so you don't run out?
- ☐ Do you find the colors and wall decor in your home and office pleasing?
- ☐ Is the temperature in your home and office comfortable?

■ PHYSICAL HEALTH

- ☐ Do you sleep 6–8 hours every day?
- ☐ Is your bed comfortable?
- ☐ Does your back feel fine after sitting in your chair at work?
- ☐ Do you eat fresh, healthful food almost every day?
- ☐ Do you exercise at least three times a week?
- ☐ Is your cholesterol count within the normal range?
- ☐ Do you drink at least five glasses of filtered water each day?
- ☐ Do you drink caffeinated drinks (coffee, tea, sodas) only on occasion?

- ☐ Do you keep your sugar-intake to a minimum?
- ☐ Do you get a complete medical physical annually?

■ MENTAL HEALTH

- ☐ Do you wake up looking forward to your day?
- ☐ Do you take the time to acknowledge what you are grateful for each night?
- ☐ Do you take at least two vacations a year that refresh and energize you?
- ☐ Do you have someone in your life that hugs you regularly?
- ☐ Do you arrive at least five minutes early for your appointments?
- ☐ Do you take your time when driving?
- ☐ Do you promise only what you can deliver?
- ☐ Do you regularly explore new ways of perceiving the world?
- ☐ Do you have a good belly laugh at least once a day?
- ☐ Do you have at least two friends outside of your immediate family who you feel free to talk with about anything?

■ MONEY

- ☐ Are you debt-free?
- ☐ Do you save at least 10% of your income?
- ☐ Do you carry at least $50 in cash to cover emergencies?
- ☐ Are you compensated adequately for your work?
- ☐ Do you recover from financial disappointments quickly, knowing things will improve?
- ☐ Do you have a savings account to cover home, car and health emergencies?
- ☐ Are you amply insured for your home, car and health?
- ☐ Do you invest in your own career development so you can earn more in the future?
- ☐ Do you have a special knowledge or skill that gives you job security?
- ☐ Do you have a reputable and knowledgeable financial advisor?

■ RELATIONSHIPS

- ☐ Do your family/friends/colleagues encourage your dreams?
- ☐ Do your family/friends/colleagues support your efforts to relieve yourself of stress?

❑ Do you avoid no one?

❑ Have you said I'm sorry to those who feel you've harmed them in some way?

❑ Do you need to forgive a family member/friend/colleague for hurting you?

❑ Do you tell those you love how much you care about them?

❑ Are you free of the need to fix other people?

❑ Are you free of people who repeatedly disappoint, frustrate or disrespect you?

❑ Do you feel significant with everyone you come in contact with?

❑ Do you have a relationship with nature, your God or a force outside of yourself that recharges your faith?

■ **Total Boxes Checked On (date)** _____

Tally up the boxes you checked.

Set goals to achieve the boxes left blank, one box at a time. Start with the category you scored the highest on so you begin on your strongest foot.

Work on this checklist until your score reaches at least 45. As your score increases, notice how much your energy increases as well.

Appendix C
STIR It Up: An Exercise in Choice

Choose a situation or person that stresses you, that keeps stealing your mind away from the present, or that can ruin an enjoyable moment if brought to your attention.

If you are using this technique alone, write down your answers.

If you are using the technique to coach others, include each step and be sure you have an agreement to take action at the end.

See the problem (state a one-sentence headline that summarizes the situation)

General examples: (details needed)
- Company/manager doesn't care
- Success is not possible
- Friend does terrible thing
- They don't understand/won't listen

Tell the story (describe what you believe is happening and who is at fault)

1. Why do you think the person/organization did this to you?

2. What are you feeling as a result?

Inquire (get to the source/reality and look for other possibilities)

1. Is the story absolutely true? Is there any other reason they "did this to you?"

continued on next page

2. What do you think was taken away from you, really?

    OR

    What are you afraid of losing or not getting? (Respect, love, appreciation, approval, control, credibility, security, accomplishment, happiness)

3. Can you ask for what you really need? Can you get it elsewhere, or give it to yourself?

4. Are you giving the person/organization what you want them to give to you? Are you willing to do this?

Reframe (state a new headline describing your position and the action you're willing to take)

- Company/manager is trying to keep head above water, employee finds way to help.

- Success is possible; I will do _____ to create it.

- Friend is taking care of himself; I will take care of myself by doing _____

- I was not willing to understand them; I will not take their action personally, as intending to harm me. Instead I will now_____.

RESOURCES

■ BOOKS

Allen, Steve. *How to Be Funny: Discovering the Comic You.* Columbus, OH: Prometheus, 1998.

Barrett, Richard. *A Guide to Liberating Your Soul.* Waynesville, NC: Fulfilling Books, 1995.

Brodie, Richard. *Virus of the Mind.* Seattle, WA: Integral Press, 1995.

Buber, Martin, trans. Walter Kaufmann. *I and Thou.* New York: Charles Scribner's Sons, 1970.

Buechner, Frederick. *The Longing for Home.* San Francisco: Harper, 1997.

Campbell, Joseph, with Bill Moyers. *The Power of Myth.* New York: Doubleday, 1988.

Childre, Doc Lew, Howard Martin, and Donna Beech. *The HeartMath Solution: The HeartMath Institute's Revolutionary Program for Engaging the Power of the Heart's Intelligence.* New York: Harper Collins, 1999.

Csikszentmihalyi, Mihaly. *Flow: Psychology of Optimal Experience.* New York: Harper & Row, 1990.

Frankl, Victor. *Man's Search for Meaning.* Boston: Beacon Press, 1959.

Goleman, Daniel. *Emotional Intelligence.* New York: Bantam Books, 1995.

Hendricks, Gay, and Kate Ludeman. *The Corporate Mystic: A Guidebook for Visionaries with Their Feet on the Ground.* New York: Bantam Books, 1996.

Mayer, Bill. *The Magic in Asking the Right Questions.* Chicago: Mayer Press, 1997.

McKay, Matthew, Martha Davis, and Patrick Fanning. *Thoughts & Feelings: Taking Control of Your Moods and Your Life.* Oakland, CA: New Harbinger, 1997.

Miller, Timothy. *How to Have What You Want: Discovering the Magic and Grandeur of Ordinary Existence.* New York: Henry Holt, 1995.

Murphy, Michael, and Rhea A. White. *In the Zone: The Transcendent Experience in Sports.* Reading, MA: Addison-Wesley, 1978.

Pearsall, Paul. *The Heart's Code.* New York: Broadway Books, 1998.

Richardson, Cheryl. *Take Time for Your Life: A Personal Coach's 7-Step Program for Creating the Life You Want.* New York: Broadway Books, 1998.

Vanzant, Iyanla. *One Day My Soul Just Opened Up: 40 Days and 40 Nights Towards Spiritual Strength and Personal Growth.* New York: Simon & Schuster, 1998.

Whyte, David. *The Heart Aroused: Poetry and the Preservation of the Soul in Corporate America.* New York: Doubleday, 1994.

Zukav, Gary. *The Seat of the Soul.* New York: Simon & Schuster, 1999.

■ Contemporary Business Magazine

Fast Company
800-688-1545
www.fastcompany.com

■ Emotional Intelligence Coaching

Pyramid Resource Group, Inc.
1919 Evans Road — CentreWest Commons
Cary, North Carolina
www.PyramidResource.com
(919) 677-9300

■ Improvisational Acting Classes

Artistic New Directions
212-875-1857
ArtNewDir@aol.com
www.improv.net

In Los Angeles — Gary Austin
800-dogtoes
wkshopinfo@aol.com

In New York — Carol Fox Prescott
www.carolfoxprescott.com

BRAIN TRAINING TOOLS ORDER FORM

Based on her best-selling seminar, Marcia shares techniques for getting to the core of productivity and communication problems — emotions — to finally create long-lasting, effective results. Give the Gift of Clearer Vision. Great for Clients, Friends, Staff and Students

■ **BOOKS BY MARCIA REYNOLDS**

How to Outsmart Your Brain: Using Your
Emotions to Make the Best Decisions…At Work $10.00 x _____ = _____
A look at how the brain sabotages our best efforts at work, and how you break-through these barriers to be more successful.

Capture the Rapture: How to Step Out of Your
Head and Leap Into Life $16.95 x _____ = _____
A practical as well as inspiring guide to reprogramming the brain for joy.

■ **AUDIO CASSETTE PROGRAMS**

Being in the Zone: The Secrets of
Performance Excellence $19.95 x _____ = _____
Learn how to tap your personal powers, how to fill in your energy holes, how to have your life feel effortless while reaching your dreams. 2-tape program + workbook.

Golf in the Zone: How to Master the
Mental Game of Golf $19.95 x _____ = _____
Success won't come from a new driver or long-flight ball. It comes from you — your mind set — your capacity to create new mental habits. Golf in the Zone shows you how. 2-tape program + workbook.

■ **LEARNING TOOLS**

Magic Paradigm Shifting Glasses: See Happiness
Everywhere You Look $2.00 x _____ = $_____
"Blow it Out, Let it Go" Balloons   Pack of 10 @ $2.00 x _____ = $_____

Subtotal = $_____

AZ residents add 8% tax + $_____

Shipping ($4.00 for 1st book/tape, add .50 for each additional) + $_____

Grand Total = $_____

Payment must accompany all orders — U.S. dollars only

Make checks payable to:
Covisioning, 4301 N. 21st St. #56, Phoenix, AZ 85016

❑ Visa ❑ MasterCard ❑ American Express ❑ Discover

Card #_____ Exp. Date (mm/yy)_____

Signature_____

Cardholder name, address and phone (if different than below):

_____

Ship to: Please print or attach your business card

Name_____

Address (no P.O. Box please)_____

City, State, Zip _____

Daytime Phone Number _____

Call for quantity discounts: 602-954-9030. Allow 2 weeks delivery.

ABOUT THE AUTHOR

Marcia Reynolds, M.A., M.Ed. and Master Certified Coach, focuses on learning and sharing new insights on how to use emotions to improve the quality of work and of life. As president of Covisioning, she brings over 20 years of experience working with a diverse set of organizations including telecommunications and technology firms, health care corporations, federal agencies and banks. Reynolds is a world-renowned coach and past president of the International Coach Federation. Excerpts from her book and interviews have appeared in *Fortune Magazine, Health Magazine, Christian Science Monitor and The New York Times,* and she has appeared on ABC World News, National Public Radio, and Japan Nightly News.